Fall

Huzefa Lodghar

Copyright © 2023 by Huzefa Lodghar

All rights reserved.

This book or any portion thereof may not be reproduced or used in any manner whatsoever without the express written permission of the respective writer of the respective content except for the use of brief quotations in a book review.

The writer of the respective work holds sole responsibility for the originality of the content and The Write Order is not responsible in any way whatsoever.

Printed in India

ISBN: 978-93-5776-916-7

First Printing, 2023

The Write Order
A division of Nasadiya Technologies Private Ltd.
Koramangala, Bengaluru
Karnataka-560029

THE WRITE ORDER PUBLICATIONS.

www.thewriteorder.com

Edited by Ridham Bassi

Typeset by MAP Systems, Bengaluru

Publishing Consultant - Deeksha

Contents

LIGHT 1

INSOMNIA 2

LION 3

POKER PLAY 4

TUG OF WAR 5

SUPERMAN 6

RANDOM 7

ARTIST 8

RAIN 9

THAT ONE NIGHT 10

THE HEART'S MIND 11

WORD'S WORTH 12

THE SUN DANCE 13

TRANSIT 15

LIES 16

TIME 17

SYLLABLES OF SILENCE 18

UNSPOKEN 19

DREAM SUPPLY 20

STROKES OF LOVE	21
FABRICATED ECLIPSE	22
THE BARGAIN	23
WOMAN	24
BLACK LIGHT	25
HAPPY BIRTHDAY	26
I'M HER MAN	27
WORK	28
INTENSITY	29
THE AWOKEN QUEEN	30
QUEEN	31
FIRE	32
FLAMES	33
FIRE RAIN	34
UFF!	35
SEA	36
SKYLESS MOON	37
SKY MIRROR	38
WHAT IS IT?	39
LOVE	41
I'LL CALL IT LOVE FOR THEE	42
HMM	43
LIFE AND DEATH	44

LAILA	45
INDEFINITE CURFEW	46
CLOWN	47
CROWN	48
UNDER DOG	49
DEVILS INCARNATE	50
CAPITOL CINEMA	51
DOA	52
PAIN	53
POET'S PAINT	54
END TO START	55
INSOMNIA II	56
POISON	57
NEED	58
ACEMETERICAL	59
DEAD LIFE	61
DRAMA	62
WAR CRY	63
DOT	64
MAA	65
COME DRESSED IN DEATH	66
COLORS OF BLACK	67
RAPED	68

GLADIATOR	69
THE FEET OF WINGS	70
I, EYE AND US	71
WITNESSES	72
HANDS OF TIME	73
WORDS OF SILENCE	74
PUNCTUATE THIS	75
REFLECTION OF SHADOWS	76
PURPOSE	77
HITCH HIKE	78
BANANAS	79
GIVE AND DON'T TAKE	80
GUISE	82
BY THE SEA	83
OMIT IF YOU PLEASE	84
THE LAST RITE	85
IN DEPENDENCE	86
LAMRON BA	87
TRIAL	88
DAWA	90
WANTS OF PAIN	91
BAREFOOT MILLIONAIRES	92
SIDES OF ROUND	93

GRAHAN	94
SCARRY NIGHT	95
ECHOES OF A DREAM	96
CATAPULT	97
FABRIC OF SOUL	98
ART WILL FIND YOU	99
LOVE THIS IS	100
POOR ART	101
NO GOD BUT GOD	102
MASTER PEACE	104
HOUSE OF HOME	105
LIE DOWN	106
CRUMBS OF LOVE	107
CRIME OF ART	108
SKY UNDERWATER	109
PURPOSELESS	110
ARAFAH	111
ONE LAST TIME	112
SKULLS OF HEART	114
DOPE	116
CONFESSION	117
LESS ORDINARY	118
RSVP	119

ACT	120
ET TU I	121
FREEDOM	122
IN SPACE, WE TRUST	123
Scent of Gutter	124
COLORS OF SOUND	125
COLD WAR	126
GOSPEL TRUTH	127
A MUSE	128
EPITAPH	129
FOOLS DIE	130
FACEWASH	131
MADMAN	132
COPYRIGHT	133
SOME EYES THOSE	134
DEBT	135
FALL	136
SHH	137
DARK DAY	138
TRUE LIES	139
SHAMELESS NOT	140
SPOILS OF VICTORY	142
BALLOT	143

BLIND COLOR	145
BOMBED	146
YA ALI, MADAD	147
MIND THE WOODS	148
FOR THE WAR OF LOVE	149
FIREFLY	150
REAL FICTION	151
SHAM	152
ART YOU READY	153
DON'T COVID THE FLOW	154
RIHAYI	155
INSANITY	156
ONE DAY MATARAM	157
ART THIS	158
MOOD	159
DARPAN	160
AKS	161
HUM	162
SEDATED	163
ALL COLORS LIFE	164
TURBULENCE	165
i AM NOT US	166
LONELY CROWD	167

FEET OF SKY	168
SOME BARK AND BITE	169
WE ARE ALL MAD HERE	170
SEVEN SHADES OF BLACK	171
A VOID THIS	172
DON'T	173
MANE MAN	174
POOR KING	175
DREAM INN	176
METRO DREAM	177
i AM	179
ART SERVICE	180
i OF THE STORM	181
LURKING	182
NOT TOLL FREE	184
PHIR SE	185
AWARA	186
PYASA	187
SANGAM	188
KAGAZ KE PHOOL	189
SHREE CHAR SAU BEES	191
DIL SE	192
DEEWANA	194

DARR	195
RAVE	196
WORLD VOID	197
WE ALL FALL DOWN	198

LIGHT

i know of a light more honest in the dark!
it sells me a dream every night...
it comes playing the tune she did the night before!
shrill enough to be heard, low enough to intrigue.
i pay her handsome, i pay her my secrets.
some naive of boyish lust,
some grave wrapped under blankets.
i trust her, so does she; we don't touch yet her i feel.
like a peddler selling substance, she vanishes, leaving me
a dream for sleep.
now drugged, i'm left alone with some random colors —
she gave me some hues of my own!
she is but a wily thug; she sold me enough to want more.
i now wait to hear that rumble again.
i now wait to see that light
more honest in the dark!

INSOMNIA

and i hear it again.
the crack when the day breaks,
the promise night made, relentlessly repeating, revolving, rotating.
i walk in hope to tire enough to drink another glass of dream
when i wake in my sleep again.
knowing it will powder again, when the day breaks.

LION

grit, valor, blood, and i move on.
in a maze, it's a haze, and i move on.
cuts, slits, pricks, and i move on.
i roar, my body's sore, and i move on.
growing old in the same mold, and i move on.
i know i'm tired, but only i, and i move on.
i scare them, they fear me and i move on.
this is my jungle. i am the king but i must move on.

POKER PLAY

i came with my pockets full to play to win,
unaware i had lost the moment i stepped in.
i couldn't control my entry, nor will i my exit, and not too much of the play either, but my
part, i shall extempore.
i will breathe pride, i will smell power.
i will wear a mask , i will use my cover.
i will seek pain, i will hide my blush as long as, at the table, it will be my flush.
i will win my wins, i will win my losses!
it will be my tracks, it will be my horses.
my hurt will be mine, and your joy too.
i will snap the shots, it will be my cue.
i will rise high, and so will my fall!
i'll lose every dime but it will be my call, my cards, my dice, my tray.
i welcome you all to poker play,
and when the masks are down and they take me out,
and when you see my eyes grin, be sure of your doubt!
yes!
they've taken me down.
they've won that round!
but will grief me those merchants of diamond, and aces of spade, and kings of club will
dig, and the queen of hearts will stray!
coz in his box, his cloth, in his own clay! the joker is now gone, so has his poker play.

TUG OF WAR

pulling it hard,
for it to come on my side.
it seemed to be in control,
but it's now beginning to slide.
my hands are ripped,
i'm losing my grip,
and my smile can no longer pretend.
it's a tug of war with life, and i so want it to end.
blood, sweat, tear—i've given it my all.
my end might be like Lear[1],
but i've lost too much too fall.

---

[1] The central figure in Shakespeare's tragedy King Lear.

SUPERMAN

the price i pay to make you believe i'm the best.
i cannot shrug, i cannot bog down, i just cannot rest.
i am just an actor. i play my life well.
it is when i have to live it, i dwell.
on the price i pay to make you believe, i feel no pain.
i cannot run, i cannot hide, i stand and wait for the rain.
a mood,
a hero,
a clown,
—i am all that you have to say.
yes! i am your Superman.
but i've had a super price to pay!

RANDOM

i come when you are not looking.
i confuse, i'm powerful.
i amuse.
i become your habit.
i make you laugh without reason.
i don't let you cry without one.
i am your smile,
i am your tear.
i choose to be unseen,
but i don't disappear.
i am your thought,
i am random.

ARTIST

a bizarre knit of snapshots in motion,
weaved with threads of
desire,
soaked in fast color, still raw and dripping.
splurge and disorient in perfect sync,
to make a picture that i paint for your eyes,
of your eyes,
bcoz they have a story to tell,
of us which i want you to read.
you can call that too a dream.

RAIN

and i smell Earth,
my mood changes from sad to gloomy.
it grows darker around me and i fear it.
it's so quiet now that i hear it.
alas! the drops hit sand,
i now know God's on my side.
i'm in love with my pain.
yes! here comes the rain.

THAT ONE NIGHT

and i shut my eye to wake up,
and i shut my eyes to wake at this huge teak of a door.
as i squeak open one side, i step into this light so dark that i black out.
i see stars hung on this house made of black marble like there is a festival they beckon.
a starry night, i must say, a starry sight, i must say!
the same stars blossom on the fields that spread further with every step.
i walk without my feet touching the ground, just enough to feel sand.
yet i know i am not grounded.

THE HEART'S MIND

and that mind goes down,
slowly in the dark to meet his beloved,
which he despises in the light to retain his supremacy!
and that mind goes down,
slowly in the dark to meet his beloved,
which he despises in fright to behold his legacy.
but that mind has a heart that knows to die in love,
though not made for it, but was destined to fall somehow.
they meet, they stumble, they falter,
just a night filled with vows to meet at the altar!
and so they keep their promise and have come to live this day!
they hold their place in light only to find a place in the dark to stay!

WORD'S WORTH

if words were sold in weights of what they meant and silence wasn't gold,
we'd have richer stories to read,
and even costlier stories to tell!
for i see too many overused words floating around, searching for the right price.
and then maybe we could talk about love,
but still this wouldn't guarantee honesty, this still wouldn't warrant time!
coz i've seen myself over spend on silence,
what would keep me from this indulgence!
but then i would illustrate the things that go in my head only coz i know they come with a cost
and then i would tell you how i see things dance, every time i wrote
about love on paper before i did fold!

THE SUN DANCE

giving shadows a shade to hide,
letting the sun slide into the seas splashing stars in the sky;
giving the moon a theater to stage her act, another night of short stories of romances,
dances, chances;
giving the wind an audience in the trees that sway in trance,
calling their gods to pour down in the streams that keep falling off the cliff unmindful of
her dreams hurting at each rock that try and bend her ways just to embrace the river
that awaits.
far across on the other side is a story that still writes of a man whose words could
never melt,
stayed put in a place scattered with times now frozen.
he could be the sun too,
he could have burnt too.
but not all that he doth have a reason.
he could be the world, but was given just a season,
a romance more gracious than grace,
and so the moon and ice live on without a vapor, without a trace...

...
don't get fooled.
he never sets;
he just finds another place to burn!
what wrong could have brought him to this penance, or has he chosen it upon himself?
must be a failed love story, i assume,
coz i've seen his art on the skies!
was he the inferno's lone artist who fell in love?

TRANSIT

hi, Dad!
everything is fine here.
the sun is a little more sober, the nights long.
i think i touched the stars, must be a lag!
there is this whole tribe here now that i am a part of, yet i feel apart!
i tried calling you, but i am not subscribed to make calls out of coverage.
the food is alright too, i miss home food sometimes; you know how much i like eating out.
there is this man who owns us all,
i think they call him God.
he has a heart; i always knew you had.
i'm lazy here too, but they say they've seen me working hard.
you know when i went off to sleep that day, the sand kinda cleansed my body up;
all the pores of doubts opened up.
i think I'll stay in this spa for a lifetime, or, should i say, for a death time?

LIES

what artist those eyes!
what truth in those lies!
make believe fables told well,
wrapped and taped ready to sell.
like a fool, it fools me, not knowing that i know i'm being fooled and how!
it's a lie and i know it is; but i can't help but love those eyes.
what artist those eyes!
what truth in those lies!
eager, almost nervous like a child, it hesitates!
unperturbed almost still it fakes,
it makes me believe; it needs me to see to show her around!
i go with the flow, i take her to places, knowing every second is not my moment to have.
yet weak and helpless, i move and move deep in those eyes.
they blamed her for the broken promises she kept, but not one eye saw those eyes
that wept.
but i've seen them hide, i've seen them wet,
i've seen hope in that playful duet.
every once in a while it haunts me to death.
was i not there when they wanted me?
did i ever shut my eyes on thee?
it still gets wet when it thinks of me, i presume,
coz every time it rains here, it brings her perfume.

TIME

time
this!
it shows on your face, in the wrinkle, at the corner of
your eye that have
soaked tears dry in hope of another day sometimes.
same like the day
passed, or in hope of a less ordinary day.

SYLLABLES OF SILENCE

i am not in awe of her,
certainly not;
make no mistake!
it's not the time i spend with her i rejoice,
i am an easy man to please,
it's just the time i spend with myself in solitary, i see her around mostly.

UNSPOKEN

you will find yourself every time in that ink that writes for me.
not her grace,
not her stare,
not even that boisterous flair...
her nude sound,
her absence,
her charm,
lied in everything she didn't say!

DREAM SUPPLY

let your heart hold the hands of your eyes.
let them go for a walk.
let them buy you food for your dreams.
let them stock!
some colors, some chalk, some that stayed behind, some you walked ahead of,
some stories that you threw out of your house,
some that sneaked out,
some that got drenched in the rains that didn't let your streets drought.
i heard they complain of a cold that doesn't go away.
let them spoil themselves, let them shop!
dreams are not made miserly,
don't ask them to stop.

STROKES OF LOVE

and what must have transpired?
what must be his plan?
he gave me you!
i am not an artist, i am just a painter; i fell in love with
the colors.
i did though love every bit of it.
i did, though, splash those colors.
they call it clumsy;
you call it abstract;
i call it love.

FABRICATED ECLIPSE

and she swivels for centuries,
unmoved like a jewel that shines like a star from far, and as beautiful and as intricate can be,
with gold fuming on one side, and silent rivers of silver flowing on the other.
not all, but there is this stream of dusk that keeps flowing like a devil meticulously common,
meticulously unnoticed, but it stays.
every once in a while even the constant changes!
just a little bit, just enough, that plunges an incomplete leap.
her sun, her moon, her dusk, cross paths merely a spectacle to bewitch the common,
to make sure the days are confused with the night,
to make sure we see the black light.

THE BARGAIN

the air back there is just a scent of what it used to be.
i give up after a few steps;
going back is not a way of moving ahead i learn!
i traded my sky for a piece of land i now own.
i was given a kingdom in exchange of my swagger!
i traded for an anvil to let go of that dagger.
age has gifted me doubt this year,
gave me that fog back which was crystal clear!
the bright skies look dubious,
i don't trust those empty roads anymore!
the nights have lost their essence,
they are just black now.

WOMAN

she brought us here; she gave us breath;
she fed her self; she gave us her health;
she became our friend, sometimes young sometimes old;
we called her sister, beautiful and bold.
We became her suitors; we pursued her like we had nothing to lose.
she yielded our child, and when that newborn smiled, we saw glimpses of her who brought us here!
what a misfortune and what an irony!
we stained, we tore, we crushed that soul, that very womb that had us bore.
if He who owns us all is a man just like me,
i wish to see his anger, his wrath if need be!
did He, who make the man, make me?

BLACK LIGHT

and what story shall i tell thee, of that black light that couldn't be!
designed for destruction, made to confuse, but did in his own blood infuse, to let not
the world demand to explain, of why it refused to shine, and be doomed to eternal disdain!
a secret story of love, if i may name it, as any other expression t'is passion would not tame it.
began to end till the end ends!
tough, did they blister magic at several bends!
they were made to live in parallel worlds and so will they!
therein lies their charm of selfish selflessness!
for who shall speak of that story if their glory got ever claimed.

HAPPY BIRTHDAY

and so he picked this day...
or did you trick your way down?
coz i've heard of your blasphemous love and how!
the flowers couldn't rub fragrance,
the butterflies lost color.
the birds couldn't chirp.
the beasts roared without vigor.
this day!
they mourn
this day...
this day, he picked, to make you.

I'M HER MAN

i'll take the brunt until every inch grunts!
and so I'll hunt for her.
and they want a new me, and so shall they get in her!
not an heir to take my legacy forward; an heiress shall i live in after all!
we don't need kings; we have seen their vain!
perhaps a queen could yeild blossom in pain!
and so shall she live my dream, and so shall she live hers too!
for she shall be her and a part of me too!
i now need time for me, for a path she shall tread.
as she grows to be her! Untaught, uninhibited, but in stead!
and so shall she learn to write all her wrongs
and so shall she learn to right all her wrongs!

WORK

churning drop after drop life chisels,
night soothes like a lullaby, every day sizzles.
it takes too much for what it gives in return, a bad bargain almost treacherous, but we learn
not to give in all at once, not to invest all we have, keep some things hidden within, beneath,
underneath that red tool of blood we call heart.
we learn to save, to hide for the drought for that night that don't sing for the rain, for the
days that don't bring the light that sizzles, unknowingly, while life is at work churning
sweat of your brow, that heart emulates her estranged twin and starts to think like him.
she reasons and then curbs her whim; like a demon, he spreads his veins of doubt.
all that love takes a heavy clout; it withers. it tithers, it finds a way out, drop by drop,
as life chisels.

INTENSITY

where did the love go?
how did the intensity powder?
bury the words; let the silence be.
louder, that silence which i picked of your eyes, every
time they looked around
searching for a place to stay,
that silence which we talked about,
when we chose to walk
steadily away.
some unfinished bits still stutter on my desk, like a fish
gasping,
waiting for one long breath
before it ends her wait to fly.
but it at least tried herself to death.
but where did that love go?
what powdered her intensity?

THE AWOKEN QUEEN

draped in night from head to toe
with just her face to show,
given company by a thousand handpicked maids
that dance in parades, rejoicing and shouting names like
carnival of blue;
the queen is woken to...

QUEEN

and the echoes of my laughter begin to fade.
and i hear the empty silences that invade,
joking as they come mocking, making fun...
ah! That fool rolls another day in vain.
faking insanity to remain in sane, all in hope to trade some solitude for some shade in that scorching light for the brief silence that stays before that encore of stupidness to buy more time.
time to paint more coats of buffoonery to hide the dull yet true colors on that wall,
to hide cracks—some made by age that have aged tactlessly, some by the rains that have cried relentlessly in a corner,
a corner picked by herself for no reason,
no season, just like her own self flowing without restraint.
mixing perfectly in the paint, i now paint,
to buy that silence that mocks me and comes
joking about, making fun at the price i pay to buy her everyday.

FIRE

and she burns too while lashing flame after flame.
have you ever heard of dry rain?
i filled a bucket from a flowing stream of fire,
i had to burn a few things to ash too.
blistering every inch that comes her way in rage,
she storms across forests, across mountains,
stashing ashes in vain.
she will never come back to pick them;
she will burn down too,
she could have baked bricks to make a home,
she could have furnaced a well cut diamond,
but she chose to take everything down to feed her unrequited desire!
o, what taste for satire! He who made water, made fire.

FLAMES

flames flabbergast, leaving burns that last...
i promise that every night that spurred light,
that raged in the caged heart, that took a beating every
time it knew you would come dressed.
for my eyes, was all but lies!

FIRE RAIN

insane pain this, ages you!
the end you caged, rages you.
but let it now begin, let there be thunder,
let the flames rain, let not even a wish meek to surrender,
let all burn down if it has to,
but don't stop the rain!
for once let her have her say,
for once let her dance away,
let her burn her hands to find out,
what gruelled more–
the fire she burned in,
or the fire she burned out!
let her trust, let her speak,
how long could she possibly have
this silent misery to keep?
let her words get a voice, corner her to no choice
where she has no story to foster.
let her write her own tale to keep;
if she has to cry let her have her own ashes to weep!
let her life be her only bait if that's what it's gonna cost her!
coz it burns time, it ages this pain so let all burn down if it has to; just don't stop the rain.

UFF!

that light which love calls herself and boasts of her radiance, not once does it strike her.
it's the sacrifice the darkness has made to remain black!
for what shine that shall make her proud
that doesn't have a night on her back!

SEA

and that light silhouettes on the bay,
kissing the sand just enough to light them up!
and the waves retire, gently dying one by one!
as beautiful as it might sound, it looks far gorgeous,
but she comes just to sprinkle the dust she was given to
cast enough spells,
not to let the dark blackout!
alas, i hold her
knowing each second is rolling not to come back!

SKYLESS MOON

they took away the skies he was under, but they couldn't take his arrogance for love.

they took away the weed that filled the pipes. but they couldn't take away the sound it made where dreams were born.

and what must have transpired in the silence i gave her? she listens not; she sees not.

SKY MIRROR

for what powers did that sky happen to show me a starless night, to show me the face of my thoughts?
they seemed all handsome until their faces showed, more like my head, that calls me beautiful, to which my mirrors fray...
o black night, with a mirror more bright than the clear skies that show the sun...
am i what i make of you? dark, unhappy, digging deep pointlessly coz it isn't common heard.
or have you forced your dreams upon me?
am i your illegitimate son that you picked for painful joy?

WHAT IS IT?

and the night bends in the streets, roaming pointlessly to seek that
light he unknowingly blanketed.
the light, on the other hand, just spills, waiting for him.
the night now, forgetting that he was made blind for a reason.
how else could he be kept apart from that moon?
and the night bends in my street, where i sit, watching from the
corner of my balcony.
the night, like an unrequited sea, knocks every time it passes a house
for a dream, a wish, a complaint, or a note.
i throw my boat of wish too.
i don't ask for much; God has been kind.
i just want to sail in those black tides,
for i seek that light too; i must be blind too.
how else could i be kept apart from that moon?
and now i have befriended this night so much that
it knows why i don't cry, it knows why i shut my eye, it knows that when i speak, i just do it to let my silence be untouched.
that's all i have left of me now,
and this night helps me meet her every time, unapologetic.
this night helps me see her every time, unapologetic.
my heart sits beside me, hanging his feet over a step, living his own unregretful life…
he sees you, talks to you, and even caresses you,
while i just mutter a few words to make you stay.

i know you don't know that he still lives with you.
he slid into your bosom when you left.
tell him he was not designed just for love.
who will pump the blood he clot?
he makes me live twice every time i live with you.
i live just not once every time.
i live with you.

LOVE

inconsistent, innocuous, purposeless love,
days mixed with dreams, nights with delusions,
delusions, so real, so true.
walks become strolls, black becomes a color,
light hates you as much as you do.
sunsets take you with them,
the moon comes back, selling its infamous drugs.
rhymes don't count; each moment is a poem.
it's there one day and not the other.
it seems unimportant, but it stays...
it is purposeless; it is love.

I'LL CALL IT LOVE FOR THEE

no name, no form, no place to belong,
yet it flows in my veins, yet it flows in the rain.
the jump, the pump, that adrenaline thump—every time
i touch you
it must be the work of God, i know, or he must come
down.
he'd have to show and teach me a different way to feel
coz every part of me that works is his bolt, his steel!
that heart i claim to be mine is his blood, that mind is his
actor, and each prop that works is his own factor!
they work in tandem, conspire magic, fool me to laugh,
and make that parody tragic!
nothing, though, is random; he must have planned this
pain.
how else can i never find peace but in her?
how else can my soul, only her sight can retain !
yet no form, yet no place, yet no name, yet no face,
but it still flows in my veins; it still flows in those rains.
i now name that rogue love for thee;
you can blame all that hurt on her all your reason to be!

HMM

and so it was named differently on different days
and so it was unnecessary in so many ways!
but it swayed, it played, and some days here that love,
and so it stayed with you some days.

LIFE AND DEATH

and it escapes in volumes of emptiness—this sound of bustling traffic, of people engaging in conversations, of useful uselessness!
each having his own agenda for talking out pains and grudges, to not succumb to this insane invite of God called life!
they come back every day to take; they come back every day to give.
like he's watching from this hole with pieces of colored glass at the other end,
they listlessly move around, adding their zing to the mundane walls, inscribing their firsts—in love, in fight!
what a sight this is, as they play along for his fetish for drama.
it looks like he has left loose ends for their story to extempore.
it clays around on its own to get molded differently on different days,
for different men in different ways;
it's the memory that they take back with them,
that shapes the building, not how it was made,
that counts, reminds you of how unmistakable this life is in trade!
for that, which was bright,
will have to find a shade,
and all that which lives will have to find a grave.

LAILA

and so she paints, with no restraints.
her thoughts, as empty as she thinks full.
random strokes fill the board, yet none can be seen.
it's her mind that paints a thousand strokes; the hand is just not as keen!
she waits and waits a whole day until it turns,
that sun, even after the dip, burns.
in that light of the moon, it shines
that fire inside fuses with that light, making it look more glorious than ever. all colors are right in front to revere!
yet she waits to paint with no restraints,
and comes a time in the day after days that pass in days.
she splashes colors and it makes art,
thus a gift she got when she left to part.

INDEFINITE CURFEW

what does hide this indefinite curfew?
a coming turbulent shrew!
i have visited this town before the houses as abandoned,
but it seems different now;
i can hear the storm coming.
the streets as colorful as i left them,
but the light has faded them enough
to give her the charm of an old world.
she was made for the nights though.
she was a festival of the gods,
but has she forgotten me?
she hasn't sent any streets to follow me today.
i did turn back!
i've been told it rains here everyday.
is it the same town that
i didn't make any promises to?
if yes, then why this rage that grew?
why this indefinite curfew?

CLOWN

why am i not your normal child?
i seek peace, and they call it wild.
why do i get to think more than supposed?
isn't my flesh brown and blood just as red?
there is a method to my madness, and it scares me.
my clown has a mind, and it tears me apart in two;
it thinks for its own,
it laughs when i want to feel pain,
it sobs in my joy.
i try in disdain to tame that sleazy toy.
throw me out, say i don't belong.
your silence is uncalled for;
i cannot hold on
scattered words,
blind song, and a muted sight.
i now fail to remember what i began to write.
why do i get to think more than supposed ?
isn't my blood brown and flesh just as red?

CROWN

and they took my crown, and pushed me down,
and wished my sweat would make me drown.
but none knew that clown, who lived in me for this day,
who jumped in joy watching me stay down in that dirt,
fighting off that rut!
but little did he know, it was my stage,
my circus,
and he too, he laughed coz he was designed to.
they took that crown coz i let them,
i staged my fall, to stage my helm.

UNDER DOG

i'll do the hard yards, I'll scratch it out!
my piece, my bits—I'll patch it out!
imperfect life this and I'll strife to keep it that way!
dreams won't sleep; i won't let that light bay!
new molds will be made, new colors born, new dough
will go in, each day newborn!
i will lose the gods and kings.
that man will have to fight!
no more pretense, no more roles played,
i'd as much scrape and bite!
as furious as he might be, no matter how sharp his claw
i will get in that dirt, i will find his flaw!
that beast will be conquered,
those fears tamed.
i'll walk, I'll limp, I'll crawl,
until that glory's claimed.
i'll use my gift of hurt, I'll make each grief pay.
imperfect life this, and I'll strife to keep it that way,
i will be not remembered as that man named God;
i'll make a story of grit, a story of that underdog.

DEVILS INCARNATE

rain me down! pain me down! decolor me, dissolve me,
just vain me down!
let the nights murk me,
let the moon mock!
let the roads throw me at every rock, let me hit
the walls blind.
let me miss turns for once!
rip every inch of me until that gut grunts,
and then I'll flow,
and then I'll rain,
and when at nights you go insane,
you'll see me in that scar!
i'll be that stain, they'll moon you about.
i'll be that black star!
the wrong incarnate, the black magic, even the devils host.
i'll just be shifting forms to be with you, i am the original ghost!

CAPITOL CINEMA

mirrors and mirage, constructed camouflage, of light that has no end.
only drawing you to her path that leads to further bends.
alluring the passersby to a feast for their eye,
taking their ears off the sound, that hustle and bustle around,
further up, the mirrors turn up,
bricked to trick you to a past in the present.
embroidered like pieces of crescent
on the fabric of truth.
those realms sparkle in your eye,
they walk you to your dreams.

DOA

amassing all that past, time roles, graying, decaying, tossing charred coals, and that which hasn't died yet burns to light the course.
it brings all it can; it brings all there is.
it brings along wrecked thrones as well as it brings along veiled corpses!
giving testimony to biases shamelessly, unjust deserved kings beg some fools in castles robust!
unfinished life, ruing to relieve, some dead rusted junk, a mirror it brings along, also it brings along a chested trunk!
time rolls and will roll you over, and so shall it!
some die in the quest to change some pick to live it.

PAIN

in pain, she stayed; in pain, she strayed!
unknowingly, she befriended that shrew;
it showed in everything she drew!
though she claimed of happiness, her breath to remain,
it was this fickle rat that pumped oil in that chain.
it is not a happy life she was after,
after all!
a short bright summer, a shorter spring, a long mellowed fall.

POET'S PAINT

it won't be a poem worth of,
if it didn't make a new painting in your head
every time you read it!
and what poet of worth you call me,
if that love in you is not a work of my ink?

END TO START

aah! that cold knife that sparked when she cut through the heart,
was mine to keep that agony,
was mine to keep that doubt.
she frisked her shoulders
to let her hair fall.
she knew I'd be there after all.
find me another way, another day to stay.
maybe, she will promise this time to break
all the vows she didn't make.
maybe, this time we will start from the end.
maybe, we'll start with nothing at stake.

INSOMNIA II

and i want the night to wait even if it's late,
and hope she hasn't thrown her bag yet,
so I can find a cigarette even if it's smoked to a butt,
coz all i need is a drag of sleep to breathe a dream.
i hope you find a shot of sleep, too.
don't but bring the rains,
i want to see you cry; bring some cold though,
i'll need a reason to burn.
come undressed of that fear and doubt that you wear;
i want to read the bare truth,
and then we may lay to live,
and then we may stay to live,
and if i lose myself, don't scream.
fool yourself again,
call it another dream!

POISON

a poison, a road, an end, an antidote, a curse in a purse,
a struggle for the worse,
happiness in pain, intolerant, insane;
a word too many, silence to remain pious in the
space, untouched, unfazed,
brutalized, even beaten by times that have eaten the spirit.
to fight, to create a room to live in denial, even if it might be; but who makes the call?
it's my breath for me to take its my sight for me to see.
for i have called light a day and
darkness night.
but do i know what it must hide
—this light in the open, or what this
darkness must have shown if it was not called the clone?
of fear, i now adhere,
but it won't be wasted; this fright,
you instilled the plot that you twisted.
i will cling on, you can pour your storm upon me!
throw me names,
call me everything dirty, but to me,
i am as God could be.

NEED

if the air i breathe has a cast, a creed,
if greed has confused need,
i recede from this race of making more gods than men,
from this race of making more swords,
to pen the pages of faith!
my days may not be bright, my nights may not mellow,
but i know the color of skies, i know the moon is yellow!
i am not colorblind, but i'm even not a racist.
i have my own purpose to find,
i am your atheist.
call me Fallen,
but i too have spent years in this life;
i too have put my all in.

ACEMETERICAL

and i write, but are you reading?
that which begins is a start or that which ends begins?
i have a bag full of questions for you,
but i don't want to know the answers;
just read them one by one!
it's not a test; i don't want to derive where you stand;
just read them one by one.
you don't have to tell me how much does a grave disturb you,
nor do i need to know how much dead can you handle,
nor is it spiritual, nor humane, nor anything to do with
changing this world around us.
i just want you to read them one by one,
and if you have lived, you must be carrying enough things
dead in you.
what does the sight of a grave make you want to do
make that one last call to say!
does it make you long for a peaceful
transition?
do you remorse all that
only you know you couldn't make right;
or does it just want you to go back to that one person?
you can use a hug of, or it just gives you happiness that all
those who have left have only left for good!
even doing nothing can be an art.
if you are allowed to,
don't you long to be with people
you want to be with amidst grave truths?
what does a blank piece of paper want to make you do?

scribble! paint! build! crush?
do it, but don't tell me!
you'll have your death just like you've had your life.
i'm not depressing you,
but if i give you a choice of dusting all that which dies in you everyday, periodically,
will it make you live longer?
don't answer me; just read them one by one!
isn't life but a collection of bits
that keep dying in us everyday?

DEAD LIFE

who are more dead—those who have gone to sleep,
or those who are sleeping?
what are you going to give back to this life,
when you are still hungry for more?
what do you want to become—a puddle of mud
that despite being dirty, can quench thirst,
or that magnificent clear sea that keeps frothing on the
shore, basking on her pride yet not a drop worthwhile?
take time to spend that time he's given you,
there are so many bodies walking around you, soul-less.
are you becoming one of them?
come, I'll take you for a walk.
can you see the graves?
they all need an excuse to come back
to make a change.
are you an heir of worth?
are you breathing reason?
come, let's go for a walk;
i'll bring silence with me,
you, get some talk!

DRAMA

and the night falls again
tearing the sky as it comes down,
enough to show the stars
enough to show the scars!
let the play begin;
a night as black as theater,
a script as dark as your soul.
don't we need a shot in the arm to sleep?
play that tragedy out in whole,
let it read word by word,
let it terrorize us with pain.
i am no lover of grief, my love,
but humor is for the sane!
for the eyes are the prettiest when moist.
we have our lips to smile.
unrequited stories adhere me the most,
coz unlike joy, they stay a while.

WAR CRY

don't you want a war?
don't you need a fight?
don't you have enough reason
to unleash that spite?
march, for now is the time to growl.
march, for now is the time to prowl.
don't just sniff, bite!
if you cannot chew, at least hurt it alright!
make a mark, live, die!
shout that gut out; it is your war; it is your cry!
and when there is no more blood to bleed,
and when there is no breath left to take,
call upon the stars in the sky, call upon that sun!
strap up, dig in, for the war has just begun!

DOT

we may have separate plots,
separate inks to write, separate blots,
different strides, maybe, different rides,
different words taking sides,
arguing, making a case,
fighting for that wrong seeming right.
it's a nasty place; this head,
nastier even his beats.
it multi tasks,
permutes,
gives you so many places to be,
and nowhere yet to go.
it loves, re-loves, re-programs
the vows it made to itself
of not leaping,
yet if
not blindfolded,
yet still,
then so be it;
it is your plot,
your ink,
your blot,

MAA

and then there is a mother,
tough words, tougher deeds,
more wants than needs,
scatter us like dust,
we keep walking, we rust,
and after a million steps,
matching shoulders with the world.
when you look back,
there is a finger that held you,
a smile that melt you.
yes, patch your bits, there is a world to win,
but there is a world, too, within—
a world full of words you have spoken,
but haven't given them a tongue,
but God knows she has heard each one of them,
coz there are people who need love to love,
and then there is a mother.

COME DRESSED IN DEATH

a cemetery is just a symbolic expression of death.
death though, like water, is colorless,
it doesn't mean you cannot add your own shade to it.
don't mourners wear black and white alike?
when i first conceived the idea of building a place upon a cemetery,
i had my own baggage of experiences, mostly emotional, grief, and sadness!
but ironically, the more i gave in,
i realized death in itself is just another state of life
we have no report on;
we are programmed to deal with it in a certain way,
like how we are programmed to deal with a toothache.
yes, it can hurt you;
but take your mind off it, and it goes!
hence, entering a cemetery would involve escaping escapism!
i'm not trying to be abstract or vague;
i intend to give you a place,
where you can celebrate loss, even pain.

COLORS OF BLACK

we are made of elements—
happiness, sadness, love, jealousy,
angst, curiosity, awkwardness, hate!
do you feel jealous when someone you competed against all your life dies; he beat you in this too? or do you feel your skin tear up into fragments when someone you're in love with dies, not knowing how you'll sun this night?
do you feel sad you couldn't confess, happy that he's gone and so has his suffering?
just a few assumptions a heart could go through,
in an event of acknowledging death!
imagine the vastness of possibilities that a mind must go through,
given that we are made, no matter how much cliched,
it might sound, unique, and amidst all this,
i give you a space where you can culture those emotions,
do the math!

RAPED

and yes, i'm guilty, and yes, i must be charged,
though it wasn't me who barged.
but all i can do is write,
which won't make a slight difference
in the way you are going to be treated from
here on.
what a pity! you were sent with a womb,
your birth, your sin, and you shall torment to your doom;
your fault, you have breasts up right,
so what if there is a heart underneath you hold tight?
of all that you wake up to, a dream you want to dawn,
you have to live a life to amuse, you are but a pawn. clean
all that blood off your torn skin, dust all that smell they
left.
it is just a rape after all, we have graver things to protest
a piece of abandoned land needs ordinance,
a river has to be told where it has to flow.
come let's take a march to wax some candles to death.
hold some pluck cards stained in red,
and get back to our dismal lives in dread.
it won't make a slight difference, these words,
it won't make a difference, these crowds;
nothing eventually will,
unless we see the beast we want to kill in others,
in ourselves, nothing ever will...

GLADIATOR

and so i step into a colosseum built of mirrors,
guarded to tame the beasts with no intention of hurting them.
i look carefully and count them one by one,
with my baited breath, my only shadow i trust.
i hear them growl, i know they must be hungry;.
sinners are gluttonous i'm told.
i wait, i let them gnaw.
they deserve to taste their master.
oh! they put on a show alright.
i know what i must do,
i know how this ends.
i hear my hand drawing the sword out,
as a smile breathes my face.
to the last drop, they shout.
to the last drop, it will... a brawl ensues,
into the dirt
as i muscle till the last drop of my marrow.
i kill everything in me to live, to become my own traitor.
as i mask another face before i step out, they must not know the gladiator.

THE FEET OF WINGS

as he strode nonchalantly to the stream to quench, after a hard day's work of nothingness,
dragging the night on his back,
while the stars dusted to sprinkle spotlight on his mane, the moon bent down to reflect, the moon bent down to remain.
far by on the edge in a corner,
reigning in her armor, his eyes met hers,
he growled, he ruffled, he knew she didn't belong.
yet a stranger guarded baiting, she stayed,
she drank, she surely was strong.
not more than a few moments of time that lapsed, she flapped her way into the skies of night.
he couldn't do too much, he couldn't let go of her sight.
behold the jungle a story ensued, they strifed their days hunting, to find nights that brewed
their hearts on fire.
in love to death,
blinded by light.
undressed of their minds and souls,
they lay there in the arms of desire.
what happens will follow how it ends tomorrow. until then a kiss parts them back into their kingdoms, where he strides into the woods to scare. she flies back into the open skies, leaving back a life in his stare.

I, EYE AND US

and yes, i was poured a storm upon.
yes, it beat me black.
yes, the bruises did hurt,
but it hasn't broken my back
yet.
for it's a far grave war that battles inside me,
a far grave truth i seek,
a far grave journey i've tripped on,
a far grave end to reach
yet.
for until now, the days have kept me company,
the nights have read pages of books
whose words light hides,
the moon often recites.
there are enough answers inscribed on the falling skies.
there are enough extracts that will rue your eyes.
are you looking
yet?
will come one day where the speech won't need words,
will come one day when the heart will dodge the ribs,
will come one day when the eyes will speak,
will come one day for me to keep.

WITNESSES

and they stare back like they know,
watching me go as i stride leaving so much behind,
taking a few deserted stones
to throw into puddles of leftover rain
that has dropped unaddressed returned desires.
towering shadows lengthening with each step,
the casts don't move, yet walk as i walk by them.
will they keep the secret or will they show
all the undoings the streets stand a witness to?
will it window?
to eyes that pry seeking to find out why,
i am my own demon, i am my own war.
i have a world to lose, yet nothing left to fight for,
who doesn't have a story inscribed on walls of unknown mansions,
who doesn't have a book of silent words,
who doesn't have a mirror that favors his vices,
who doesn't have an alibi in the name of God.
how many faces am i left with to wear?
how much time will time take to tear?
how much age will i have to grow before i take that walk to go?
sculpted magnificently by him, such deformed his art. of all he let me be, i became a heart.

HANDS OF TIME

i've walked back and forth,
and i've moved the hands of time
just to find a glimpse of that moment
when i was all you saw,
i was the sun, i was the moon, i was the sea you marooned.
won't come that time again; i know, won't come that love that showed in the twinkle of your eyes,
which wrote pages in my book they called poetry.
i let go of each breath in hope that i won't have to breathe again this air
that does not bring the smell your sound mustered.
oh love, the seed of all wars i fight inside me,
leave me.
there is nothing left for you to eat to empty.
she has kept my heart, you, my soul;
my breaths are in debt,
all that remains is a heap of sand.

WORDS OF SILENCE

she sneaks in like a lost poem;
she sneaks in right under my arm.
like a breath taken underwater,
her eyes are as fiery as yours,
her words rest on my chest like the thrust of your heartbeat.
she sneaks in like the moonlight
that bounces off a crack, leaving her trails in dust.
she sneaks in like a lost tribal,
searching for a new home.
she sneaks in like a page of history,
playing to a full theater.
she sneaks in like a melody that stirs storms in my eyes.
this loneliness, just like you, sneaks in;
it will kill me, too, but i know, but won't take this life.

PUNCTUATE THIS

some masks with eye holes,
some eyes on the wall,
some words scribbled in inscription,
some fragrance of that moonlight,
and that about all
is all i'm left with in the room
where i couch on the rest i need.
i don't intend to chase that light anymore,
if it's there it'll find me i've been told.
meanwhile i intend to get some sleep.
the darkness beneath the eyes needs to go.
the dream needs more canvas to limit the outstretched rainbow
with seven times more love than she thought there was,
with seven more words the mind spoke before it, opened its fist to let her go.
i wasn't told love was a sentence that needed punctuation to graduate.
was love ever a complete story told till date?

REFLECTION OF SHADOWS

but a room full of unidentical twins,
blurred, stirred, drenched in their whims.
i look but cannot see who has my soul,
where is that me?
i hid in a bid that auctioned souls.
i had to dress up, i had to poker roles,
and now the time has so passed
i do not know what's farce,
that which i am or that what i see.
i bred an army off my blood,
yet not one like me.
yes, them mirrors reflect me inch by inch,
i drill pass their flesh yet they do not flinch.
a product of my arsenal, a clone of my deed,
a new one reflects each day a new dog of an old breed.
i could sleep nights like a pauper with a tattered burnt sole,
but how can i sleep in a kingdom of corpses under the heaps of my burnt soul?

PURPOSE

it resonates like a vowel of silence—this emptiness.
all that is left behind in the quest to seek the man inside
rolls like the scape of a film.
a collage knit of strolling sinned nights,
scooting days in scorching soul stirring light,
of more wrongs than right, thus far.
knocking on soul after soul,
face after face,
heart after heart
to find refuge, to find a roof to rest.
the charm, though, gets me a pass,
but it doesn't last the stay as i lay undressing all that shine.
i've made up to smother the scars time has drilled unapologetically.
but i rob a souvenir from each soul that lets me in even for a short while in their inn,
and fill my bag of emptiness.
and i move on in the quest to seek
only to see within.

HITCH HIKE

said the road, don't complain,
the lane you take may have more curves than bends,
ride the bumps and make amends.
grit star glazed in scars,
a fallen star shall guide your end,
miss a few turns call it free will,
hitch hike strangers in the name of cheap thrill.
and if our roads may ever cross,
throw me a smile off that lips.
i'll wink a glance on those hips,
and we shall get back to
stroll on board, our bearer of secrets,
our witness of sins, our well of skulls, the road.

BANANAS

i've been hearing fragrances, smelling sounds,
watching silence take rounds in my veins that are now consumed by it.
twisting the lines of work, my hands now have begun to sing,
my calves have caught a flight and my feet have worn a wing.
my skin now sees all the lies that grow on trees.
my fingers now drink knowledge and throw up in a sneeze.
how will it make sense what you read
that which i write is but a work of my knees.

GIVE AND DON'T TAKE

let's light a revolution you and me.
rope, soil, oil and fire;
let's burn into smoke, you and me.
we but have our bodies, our chalice.
let's retain that vapor, you and me.
the time is tocking faster than her mark.
the days are hastening into the dark.
yes, we are moving forward but in circles,
turn around and you might hold your own sleeve.
and that which you are ploughing is your soul,
ready to reap.
come, let's build a revolution you and me.
make hate more charitable,
let love be sold for free.
we have bowed enough heads in prayer.
let's hold hands to bring down that night,
tear open the sky to make room for that light,
brow down enough sweat to water a mirage,
stir our dissimilar blood to paint a collage,
tear in a symphony to damn the barrage
of all that which you breathed but couldn't let go.
let's bring our own boats and begin to row,
for i don't intend to take you to the rainbow.
i want to show you where grits are made
and where you can buy that dough,
for we have been thought to romanticize tomorrow
and keep looking behind on the day passed.

i want you to work today for today
and leave the prints for a cast that will come here today, tomorrow.
life in the end is but what you give and what you don't borrow.

GUISE

i fill my pen with oil, wishing the friction it makes
when it words another story catches fire.
i want the words to burn down when i'm done,
caught between wanting an audience and not wanting
them to see at all that which churns in the mines of this
heart.
but i write about my plight of showing people enough
gray
that they don't think i'm all black and hiding enough black
to still walk clean in the sheaths of light.
oh life! Are you this difficult in the next house?
or is this world moving just enough so you keep your
aches right here?
c'mon, let's talk it out.
show me the end; i might just change and mend my way
of kicking you
right below your nose each time you ask me to doze off
another night.
so what if my brain ticks on a lightless day?
so what if it's just a trick?
my mind is now in love to play; let the farce pass.
we might just catch up in the grays of my time,
and yes, i will have a bucket full of regrets and your
untimely warnings.
for now, sit beside me, take a sip, and watch me make
a riot of this silence until i find your friend who loves
you enough to suck you out of each living thing it comes
across—death.

BY THE SEA

given my fate, if i were brought back to where it all started,
i would pick it up again without a flinch.
too much has passed: time, drought, cold, hurt, and the agony of having nothing at all.
what have we become?
wrinkles, dried tears, unkempt eyes, sour words—all sprung out of the seed of love? should mere love have brought us here? all that said peace unwrapping into a fit of restlessness, torn between the liberties of that heart and the grounds of mind, i breathed a breath too many.. but ask the life that knows is death bound, gasping in to savor a memory to live upon death, could it be calmer and more resolute like how we've known her to be? i am dead, but it hasn't killed me yet. i'll strap up and see you on the other side, maybe (by the sea).

OMIT IF YOU PLEASE

we buzz on purpose, we buzz in a herd,
we buzz gnawing into the day, shouting yet unheard.
we hustle and we bustle into the noise of our sweat,
selling night upon night in an auction for that dream,
for a place called nowhere, for that dream called a dream.
stacking, racking, hoarding stashes of our work
in molds of paper, land, gold,
all we gave birth to, all we are now after.
in this race to the start, the smiles have become a laughter
to impress our soul into believing all that we do is right,
and our right to right.
we thus have lost our shade of uniqueness in the same indifference of life.
we could have flapped into the color of a butterfly.
we could have moved like the seas,
yet we buzz in a cluster to produce abundance of nothing,
we buzz on the hive like money bees.

THE LAST RITE

and what is left of the last rite i now begin.
it may take some time, this burial,
the little left is all the right i couldn't exercise
in fear of war that fights within
that which needs a reason to trespass.
behold, we are all carrying wars within us,
we don't want this world to end before its end.
make use of the nights to soothe the soul
that keeps burning to light the moon.
fool yourself, you are your buffoon.
listen to strangers, monks, priests,
they always have a remedy to tame the beasts.
you won't tame them, i know;
the beasts are called beasts for a reason.
they are soldiers of the edge,
don't hold them for treason.
life will give you enough chances to die.
do you have it in you to lie,
to call famine, bloom;
to call suffocation, room?
he alone will go on to live,
he who is when put to lie,
will wake up to say it was a bloody lie,
this life was death, you fools,
i am alive now in my corpse, in my skin.
will you ever, ever know he who goes, goes out,
or goes in?

IN DEPENDENCE

nothing wrong in blooding the soil
that gave you form off your sweat.
nothing wrong in giving air to the air
that lets you breathe.
nothing wrong in owning up to the mistakes of your land.
nothing wrong being taxed for a handful of sand.
nothing wrong in shutting your eye being robbed.
nothing wrong not finding your feet in the mob.
you have been numbered like stock.
you have to stick to your herd.
nothing wrong if your scream's,
wrists are cut to be left unheard.
nothing wrong in pledging a vote into the hands of the corrupt,
and hiding in your blankets waiting for it to erupt.
nothing wrong in hoisting flags to show you are free
in a land
where even the trees have to bark down to paper to plead 'don't cut me'.

LAMRON BA

what are we but disabled souls
looking for a spark of   smile to fill the cracks time has worn.
it is time we move on and treat His children sent with a purpose
how we would want ourselves to be treated by him.
it's all about blurring the lines we have drawn. shouldn't our heart resonate as many times as their mind does?
aren't we, who treat them differently, the disabled?

TRIAL

this life will take me, just like it has a million other times, to the end.
but you know what? i will have to come back,
for as senseless, as shameless it may sound.
i love you, and it's not coz i am in a more secure space where i have nothing to lose,
not coz i am a loose man who needs it to fashion.
i do not love you to keep myself occupied.
i love you against the will of each breathing and dead part of me.
find peace in knowing that you have someone to be in love with you until time can escape into a pause,
and it doesn't even matter if you do not love him back.

right from the unsureties of fate, to having kept faith,
from random collisions of chance to the planned repercussions,
from having two pairs of identical eyes (choose to disagree) to diverse almost like the ends of the world mind,
from having to live twice to playing disappearance,
from being the most mature to out right buffoons,
from having the liberty to speak out of turn to having nothing to say at all,
if this ain't it, find me another name for love.
drama, i forgot to mention, that which you played and that which i wrote.

DAWA

what holds this breath? i cannot let go off!
will there be more left? i have a few stories to end.
death shall consume all that which lives, no doubt, but i have a few strings to mend.
abused by drugs, used by thugs,
i now float in tranquility, some space that i breathe,
and it hurts, but by God, this pain soothes more than a song!
do not correct me if i'm wrong.
let me take the alias of sickness to spurt the truth...
most of them are not listening,
and those who are wont know
and those who know won't speak!
ugh! this cold.
it has taken more space in my skull than the air
that doodles dream, pain, i like, don't mention it!
but how much more will i be consumed?
is death now the cheapest medicine i can afford?

WANTS OF PAIN

look, know that the frivolities of my words are just a pitch
to keep you engaged in my circus while i plough my plight,
there lies my fodder for the day that will come tomorrow,
for the day that will never be.
on the inside of inside, germs peace;
the fight i fight with my fears, tells me there is hope,
for only until you are not resting awaits rest.
i do not believe in a start beyond end;
there must be, if they say so.
there will be, i know, but for now, i want my mind to burn
so much in flexing room for absurdities,
that i rub every inch of strength in my muscles to combat
the darkness
that i spade to cover the hole that brings light.
let there be light; let it have its night; i will forge my night
to its day.

BAREFOOT MILLIONAIRES

frothing like bubbles on the film of life, breathe aspirations,
the strong ones budge and wait for the storm to pass,
the frivolous, drenched in exuberance, fly to fade away.
the ones left behind hold hands find similar dreams to hitchhike
to make room for as many hearts
that have beaten all odds through thick layers of tar to find light.
but a chance to find their poise in the loud,
but a chance to become a cloud; most of them will.
great leaps are often made without baggages of expectation.
sit back and give their eyes a sight.
they've been brought unreserved.
their resilience is their might.
they will one day join hands; they will one day rain.
their dreams are forged in fires of hunger; they are built on bricks of pain.

SIDES OF ROUND

we all try,
don't we,
to beat the hours of despair,
the rusty edges of night?
at some point,
we have all bled
our fingers,
we have emptied
our eyes
to look beyond,
to tear.
we are all we've got
in the end.
a couple of nights,
a day,
many lives,
heart of a woman,
will of a knot,
dreams, a tray of ice,
soul stuffed on junk;
we will pass
like that storm.
don't dwell,
all else
awaits,
maybe
on the other side.

GRAHAN

aisa nahi ki usne chua nahin tha
mohabbat do tarfa thi janaab
usne yun saans li begoshi mein
ki humari saans halak mein hi reh gayi
ye ab kaisa khauf chala hai
tum me, mujh me
jab mohabbat ki thi
to kya khaak zinda the
dur rehna hi zindagi ka mansooba tha
tujhe aaj pata chala hai
hume shuru se ilm tha
ki ab jab dekhogi
us chaand mein daago ke chinte
samajh lena ki aaj
phir se kalam uthayi thi
aaj phir sihayi
ne aasman ko
raat sa rang diya hai
bus ab yun hi milna hoga
tu chalak na chandni si mere jharoke mein
main utrunga suraj sa
teri peshani pe
aur kabhi yun hi mile kisi raaston pe
to grahan ka tika zaroor laga dena
tujhe nazar na lage!

SCARRY NIGHT

come in,
turn off the lights,
i said.
the sky,
desperate
to rue with me
dimmed
into a quiet night.
it better be a new one,
she insisted,
your story
just makes me moist,
makes me weep instead!
this has been going on for
sometime now.
we both are equally broken
and unsure, i think.
she, with her stars,
i, with my scars!

ECHOES OF A DREAM

and the echo of whispers
in locked rooms
corrode the bounties
of grief.
silence breathes,
waiting
outside the shutter.
sleep is about to draw!
a dream awaits
on the other side
of promises
that couldn't keep their word.
a world outside,
a world in a world.
is it a silent dream
or am i asleep in my words?
will you tell me
when the dream's over?
but first,
are you even awake?
are your third world problems
more intriguing than mine?
does your unpaid electricity bill
override my pain
of not knowing what color
to paint the night, tonight?
black
or black?

CATAPULT

i've been pulling all that undoing of time
and her allies on my catapult of endurance for a while now,
not wanting to let go.
what would i do without all that pain?
i can frisk the sling and shoot it away...
but i need my pain to stay inside me...
to burn me each day for a night to char another page,
for another story i build in my mind,
and pray that very second untrue.
for if he indeed washes all my grief away,
what would burn me, turn me, churn me,
what would eat my life away?
not that i am chasing an end,
not that i don't want to mend all the hearts,
i've let burn alongside.
i scream inside about how i want the wind
to blow away the dust of my words, off my words,
and how i want the bitterness in the shade to fade away.
i can pull two clouds and make it rain.
i can wash all that past away,
but what will i do without all that pain?

FABRIC OF SOUL

there is nothing more engaging than the fabric of man
—how a man finds a world in one person
and how he remains alone in that same world.
don't take me for a fool.
when i laugh with you, i am counting your tears.
you may hide your masks behind your face,
but you cannot hide from me your fears.
i stalk, and while you talk,
i am already walking down behind your secrets,
right down to their shadow.
i have spent a life doing nothing,
and there is no one more dangerous
than a man who does nothing.
i know what i don't know, which confuses me
with what i don't know i know.
it's perplexing, isn't it?
i wish i was more mediocre than this.
i have a brain that rests in unrest
and a heart all over my bones.
i can taste each one of your stinks.
i am with me, and we are all alone!
i let go of a whole world in a breath,
and in a breath, i take back the whole world.
but an ordinary life of lives i live,
with a less-than-ordinary soul.

ART WILL FIND YOU

abandoned, so alone that you become a stranger.
when you wish your eyes could speak more than hear,
when you want to bleed so profuse that it empties you,
when you want to just cry behind closed eyes,
when you set fire to the world
and wait for the ashes to bring some color to your song!
when you paint and paint till that poem sounds all wrong,
when you are ready to give your demons a world, art will find you!

LOVE THIS IS

truth, like love, transcends, transgresses,
plucks your veins out if need be,
but finds a way to flow!
from the womb of the devil to the ribs of God, truth survives all.
truth, like love, glows.
there is a life of love, and then there are days that span a lifetime.
either way, love rules over us like truth; love slows death.
it keeps it from coming, but it kills you until then, all the time.
you cannot befriend this haze; you cannot adverse her scent.
love, like the eternal plague, shall consume you all the same!
those who breathe in, those who cannot!
love will give you a life each time you die
and then beat you to death.
and then there are stories of love that haven't tasted grief or hurt!
do not bring those shabby tales to me
and do not call them love at all.

POOR ART

a simple sacred secret,
an unready truth,
a trying lie,
a life in guise of life,
grief giving birth to an alibi;
art, they say, is pain
everything it touches,
must cry
a sonnet of solace,
a painting of peace.
the wise suffer with the artist,
the fool gets amused
and passes by.

NO GOD BUT GOD

let's try,
fly,
lie
of chances
to dance
one more time
to the music of life,
move to strife,
drawing pain
on canvases,
making
verses
of poem
in white nights
that won't dawn
unless you run the moon
into emptiness,
oh world,
don't wait
for continuity,
carry on with your lives,
my nights take more days
than the sun takes
to burn light.
fight
one more round
before going down.
let the dirt be my prize;

bruise my victory,
make a note in history;
there was a man
as God could be.

MASTER PEACE

and i resolve
to solve
the wars i'm fighting
within,
the demons
that ain't biting
dust,
yet
to reform,
to sin,
to become,
to win
not a race,
but space
to place
my dreams,
as i leave another day
to reach the sun,
to burn,
to earn
enough work,
to kill the heart
before the mind dies.
It will take all the spoils
of war,
every piece
to sweat tears of blood,
to become a *master peace*.

HOUSE OF HOME

don't flaws make a house, home?
where but your walls can you confide?
where but beneath your roof
can you hide
that chink in your armor
to remain the super man
you've made people believe
you are?
no matter how far,
how pretty that paradise may be
that which you left for,
but can anyone put you to sleep
like the pillow
that has taken the brunt,
has hidden your dreams
that has heard your sound
amidst the screams,
the chaos
your mind has fogged,
the fire, the fuel, the log
of hell
which has kept you warm
in this cold night?
your grief, your weakness
work like cement in grit;
flaws make a house, home
that laughter in the audience
must've cried alone!

LIE DOWN

if i don't write,
if i don't let you in,
i may never be able to leave
this dream,
this so called life.
there are rooms in my house
that tell stories;
i hear a lot of laughter,
yet the walls are never dry.
there is so much the heart has weighed,
yet not much to cry.
there must be a seepage somewhere.
my eyes may have been blind in love.
but the smell of dried grief don't lie.
go away now,
let me be,
let me write,
let me lie.

CRUMBS OF LOVE

love transcends in poetry,
poetry transcends into art,
art speaks stories of pain,
pain draws back to love.
nothing more crazier,
nothing more true,
if there is a God,
and i know he is,
for he has left a syllable
in every gospel,
he has left us a crumb of clue.

CRIME OF ART

slaves of education,
prisoners of gratification,
students of sanity
—where do we go then
but become nomads,
live in the garb of art,
and without luck, we may become
mixing colors,
hoping to create a world
where truth can survive,
art, though, is
not just science of rhymes,
nor an industry
structuring dreams.
art is the truth inverted
a reflection
of unacceptable perspective,
a revolt against nothing,
but the demons you feed.
art, like love,
is best served crumbling.

SKY UNDERWATER

a rusting wish
set afloat in a sea of dreams.
maybe, there is a sky underneath
where birds of heartache fly
in search of grief,
where stories of silences
moisten the leaves
of lost love.
maybe, there is a jungle
of rasping wilderness
of unmanned sighs
hidden, left,
yet not disowned.
maybe, there are stones
of sorrow
unmined,
left to be discovered
in desperate times,
when only a shot of pain
can keep you alive.
there is a sky underneath
the sea of dreams
where a man is drawn alone
with all his selves
to breathe, to be...

PURPOSELESS

a heart, scars, scars, and scars...
a night, stars, stars, and stars...
the heart hides,
the night tries,
desires know no lines,
even the night, each night,
runs out of skies.
two lives
—one ours,
one mine,
so much truth
to talk about,
yet i paint lies.
love awaits those
who despise,
for those who are in love
have already paid their price!

ARAFAH

burn! He said,
and i shall save thee from fire.
climb towards me,
take a handful of sky,
drink if it rains;
do not complain
if it's dry.

ONE LAST TIME

it always starts with the eyes,
like a myth
love survives,
like a potion of magic
of all things tragic.
love thrives
in different timelines
in a dream.
you wake into
every time you sleep.
love drives
you not only insane,
but also to your beloved,
close enough.
to breathe her scent,
to watch her lie
in arms not mine,
love cries
with me
each night;
each night
love tries
to untangle the stars,
to clear the skies,
to show me her face,
one last time;
one last time,

it breathes
before it dies,
one last time
again...

SKULLS OF HEART

confined to infinity,
the heart takes a leap
into the ocean of love;
it might not outlive
the life of a firefly,
but it tries, and how
toward the bay,
it though shines
like eternal peace,
like a gateway
to the heavens,
it still is a mirage.
she will know.
only when she pays
with every muscle of her breath,
will she know
this ocean is not a road to reach,
these waters won't take her away.
she has flipped,
taken the dip,
she will thus succumb.
it won't kill her;
this love, she will live on,
numb watching other hearts
diving each day,
frothing to reach infinity,
frothing their way
into the heap of skulls

of a hundred hearts,
undead
of another hundred hearts
like flapping sea gulls.

DOPE

like someone's lifted a mountain off my chest,
or sun pouring down like summer,
or a breath of rain giving birth to a new fragrance,
like someone handing over bricks
to begin to rebuild my dream,
funny, how hope hides until
stars trip over storms.
riding the waves of wind,
dancing in front of you,
desires soaked in pain,
wriggling out of shackles
to join them.
oh! love,
i knew you could be dead,
but never gone.
passing
trespasses of barbed truth,
it takes a flight again—
all those planes
made of empty papers,
of poems.
my silence sang
this hope.
oh! this hope,
until time ends,
my friend,
my enemy,
my only God-damned dope.

CONFESSION

an imaginary prison,
an ethiopian parole,
a tender heart
weighed by grief,
a mind suffering
manifold,
aging lines of fate
giving face
to impending deeds,
lurking whips of faith,
a cilice tied to
my soul,
freedom, i now know,
is not flight.
fight, perhaps
penance too,
but for the sins
not yet done,
for the sins
i know
i'll do!

LESS ORDINARY

don't bring me good looking people;
they all look the same.
bring me a face that has a story
of broken wings,
and a life to fly
of war wrecks
that have survived.
bring me the light
of a longing eye,
a smile built in odds,
tears in hollow cries.
there is nothing more endearing
than the pathos of lines
that which age on you,
that which measure time.
perhaps, i seek beauty,
not magnificent,
not ravishing;
an ordinary story i dare seek.
i but seek a face like mine!

RSVP

what could it possibly be?
unfolded life laid down encrypted with no key
but an overdose of underused love.
we take the fall and never touch the ground.
hanging, watching stars and tides exchange pain,
hearing the moving story of water that flows but remains...
each night of nights and nights of days,
overlooking the light,
the sun rays making all black and white smear into grays...
unrequited, i must say, his ways of keeping us on the toes, in a haze.
cling on to all that you think is yours today,
for tomorrow, you may wish to live a certain way.
but never get a chance—not a dime, no way.
it works like clockwork.
all that you think chaos.
he holds the string, he holds the god damn plays.
succumb to reign, cut the chase.
you are you outside and on the inside, whichever mirror reflects your face.
there is no psychosis; there is no one but you.
all your masks are invalid.
only straight roads in this maze...
welcome, welcome, welcome... to the life of death,
and her simple, simple ways.

ACT

i feel like someone has taken off the lid.
i see birds fly out of my heart.
a little late, maybe, but nevertheless, it is a start.
can someone rip my chest too,
take the broken ribs, and clean up the bloody residue?
i wish to rebuild again, rebuild on that long-gone art,
but will insanity alone sell?
don't we need a little truth too to tell?
for truth, it looks the part of a flabbergasted lie.
i wish to paint and disguise .
serve it charred but not hot,
for if i put you in a spot, you'll leave.
who will listen to me?
believe that i am the lone God-man.
i am the only hope.
i am the world you are tiptoeing on; i am that tight rope.

ET TU I

Come hither,
go on a rampage,
there is a story lying
that never found its stage.
You can take that script too.
Let the words find her due,
for the thought is way bigger than me,
the plot is way bigger than me.
And then, untie me,
let me fly.
If then i die,
i die.

FREEDOM

that which holds you,
becomes your master.
tie a kite to your jealousies.
watch it fly away,
blow into your pain,
cry away.
give your hope a wing.
show them no branches to rest.
let them soar and sore.
let them find no nest.
give what you need the most.
power, perhaps, lies in peace.
don't invest in a dream,
take it on a lease,
evolve, become, seize.
guilt, hate, agony,
long gone despair,
cut them loose,
free 'dem.
maybe, alone then
you will find your cause.
maybe, then you will find
freedom.

IN SPACE, WE TRUST

the melody of truth is unmatched.
the lies can orchestrate a symphony to its will,
but just a string of truth can ring a bell and resonate
those empty walls of temples where gods breathe.
this love, this truth, this nudity of bliss,
sometimes lie in the blank spaces
between the words we read.

Scent of Gutter

and like the gutter, it stinks,
me thinks.
this mind, in its company, not bound by a soul,
no rigmarole of sweating flesh building a world
where my demons prey on neglected virtues.
now comfortable in this dirt, i walk tiptoed
not wanting to wake the long asleep road
that once took me to crowds,
that knelt and bowed and begged with no grace and how.
it has made me an atheist, but i haven't become one yet.
no wars end in joy, mine, for certain, won't.
between pleasure and peace,
between false and truth,
between all that wrong and right,
this fight has just begun.
coz, it may have turned me numb,
it might have choked my breath,
but know i am just asleep;
i am not dead, yet.

COLORS OF SOUND

have you heard the sound of colors?
red: the magician beats like a drum;
green: more suave, blows like a trumpet;
yellow: glorious like a crisp flute;
black: beats like the silence between the notes of a piano, and some choruses here and there;
in violets and purples and hues of whites: they sing along the play, their pieces, some in turn, some jump. they crack a melody, sometimes even croak.
but they are all out there in their symphony.
put your ear on a canvas, tell me can you see the colors of sound.
it's crazy what you've read up till now,
it'll only get crazier when i tell you all this confusion: this plague, this grief on your plate is served just enough to get you back here tomorrow,
coz happiness, i'm capable of buying and plucking from random souls;
it's the forlorn stories that your eyes bring I'd never afford.

COLD WAR

countless wars leave home.
countless wars return to sleep.
countless wars die.
countless left behind to weep each day.
most draw a stalemate, laugh, find a joke in the crowd,
belong, to be deceived.
few take back their losses, their hurt back home to grieve.
they are all wars, make no mistake,
but many of those who fail to seek within, often cut loose.
they step into battles, not theirs;
acquiring potions, not theirs; taking lives, eventually theirs;
scratching for a sign of validation in our souls, not theirs.
and so, this is how it has been played, plays and will.
there will be as many wars losing trail
as many as there are within.
which war do you want to be a part of?
what will you choose
if you believe you have enough fight for a war,
believe you have a whole world too within you
to war!

GOSPEL TRUTH

the words will have to seek forgiveness,
wait their turn to find a sound, a visual.
can any lamp ever compensate for the light the sun burns?
let's hold onto the gold in our silence,
for it will take a world to go around
to find a syllable, to even punctuate the slightest shimmer in the blade of that sword that could have killed all it chose, had it rose that day,
but destiny had it, so did his will.
he had to give his life for faith to live.

A MUSE

will they ever know the sanctity of my fears?
they but rinse the qualms of doubt.
that which remains is directly proportional to the deeds my hands,
tongue, and mind have undertaken unto others, unto me.
i thus want to live a fearless life of fear.
i but want the freedom to laugh at death.
i but want the freedom for my tears.

EPITAPH

come empty me full.
i am done half-living; i am done with half a death.
burn, decompose, throw the residue in the open air,
let someone catch a sneeze of this flair
that couldn't read enough to write more flair,
that will floor once the winds pass.
alas, shall i read my own tombstone?
the man who was dead in life has now taken the walk
to go into the woods called nowhere
with his handful of emptiness with his handful of flair.

FOOLS DIE

go find yourself some pain, you fools,
who have filmed layers of deception on your skins. make
your pulse tick, cut your veins,
ooze that blood out, burn matches,
fire your heart.
don't be in this constant need to be comfortable in joy.
look, learn, pray to forget.
find a black spot in the open skies, call it yours.
search for it every day you wake in your bed.
store your dreams in it,
but please dream.
do not waste a single night of sleep sleeping,
and once you enter your dreams,
don't disappoint gods by attending choirs and masses. rip
open the gut, let the demons loose,
and hope and pray they rub on to your hands.
the sickness consumes you one day.
that day, you will begin to live that day;
you will have taken a walk towards death.

FACEWASH

and he washes his face again and again in hope to dust. last night,
this man named High now finds company in drugs to remain sane;
his house, built in a lane where pain blooms no matter how far his walk takes him,
he has to return to his room, also called a fight by his friends.
this man hustles to bustle a breath of peace to save enough dough to buy a house in the street close to the shrine that has the names of godmen engraved.
he wants to take the path their stories have paved.
were they men who became gods or did God himself stoop down into a man?
will someone from the dead come and tell him about life back there?
his penance, after all, was a bug incepted to limit his urge to find another street full of inexpensive, made-up joy sold to stomach his hunger.
will the roads ever cross? only the end will show him the start, and like those all gone, his words will leave the throat, enduring to speak but won't part.

MADMAN

and we saw God—at least i did in his eyes.
a man, i have now seen enough to not call him a stranger, stands at the corner of a street, religiously doing nothing.
our eyes meet often, and each time i shy away after a glance.
i do not owe him an explanation for my being, nor does he ask for one.
then why do i see my years flashing back in his eyes?
why does his stare stir my spine?
is a mosque, a shrine, or a temple vast enough to behold his grace?
are we not vessels of his overflowing soul?
if yes, then why do we have to rub our foreheads to hone our lines of fate?
what should the need to seek him be?
isn't there enough God in both you and me?

COPYRIGHT

i am not here to start and end wars.
i am here to take part in this battle, to die nameless, faceless
like my brethren, in my will to hang on to a page of anonymity in history.
therein lies my identity in confusion, therein lies the fodder of the search for your tomorrow.
yes, i will tell you stories of kings and failures of soldiers and saviors.
you will, but, have to choose your part to play,
to change the plot to go astray.
i will make my ink-rut words into a mirror for you to see, to become, to be.
do not, but, burn out another draft of this god-forbidden recluse;
this world already has one me.

SOME EYES THOSE

some eyes those that smelt like a stream fresh of newly sprayed waters.
some eyes those that held hands while i walked into the darkness in search of the start.
some eyes those that fluttered pictures of life we would later make a dream of.
some eyes those so worn to all that was lost to the spoils of war,
those that showed no sign of recent dampness yet beat me empty into believing about a river holding enough to flood a sea but won't flow.
some eyes those that i know have done nothing wrong have withered before time.
some eyes those that i know could have been mine,
eyes that had a heart to dream.
some eyes those that still smell like sprays from fresh streams, every time i walk by them.

DEBT

the sun walks back into the dark, having burnt a sky on its back.
just after it takes a dip to shrug off the sweat of his day, i walk past his footprints.
as i drag down the curtain, the moon awaits her cue to begin her act,
to play out another episode of that drama called Hope,
to the ruing dreams that loiter searching for a place to rest, nesting another bait to bring light to their fight.
meanwhile, as i get taxed for the breaths that leave me, i'm forced to ponder what must have been his story:
the sun that just called his work a day now leaves to burn another sky.
what must have dawned on him to incur this debt that he now works in shifts to give light?
oh, love, oh, light, what a beauty your plight.
they burn turn-by-turn unrested to pay their debt of love, whilst this world these eyes play along to work their own debts;
they play along and how.

FALL

come, cover me up with your sins.
come, take away what's yours.
rake them leaves that did fall.
those that couldn't cry, take them away.
that's not my body lying there;
i'm up flying with the winds.
that's my heart,
my bones,
my flesh.
my mind's gone up in the infinite.
i am now what i want to be.
i've never felt this weightless before.
my soul's dead now.
like your eyes that saw but couldn't see.

SHH

what can make me write now?
i think it's a dark well my words draw me into.
who would want to stay in such a place for so long? But if it's the only place?
my words, but, are still, a third of all my silence speaks when no one is listening.

DARK DAY

so dark is the closet, even the mirrors here don't reflect.
don't come in yet, the light you bring
might shine on all that i don't want you to see.
there are no surprises,
but i don't want to see your eyes see all that i have seen.
i know you must be blessed with a room too.
i don't know what you must have call it.
i'm sure you have a heap of scars, too, you hide.
i'm sure you have your sack full of falls.
but are you as lucky as me?
do you, by date, remember each undoing upon you
by yourself and those you let?
is your rendezvous with hell as chronicled as mine?
so dark is the closet of my mind,
that just the thought of light makes it creep.
close that door on me when you go;
the light you got might still shine on all that
i don't want even me to see!

TRUE LIES

and so i've rubbed my nose in the sun a few times.
a few times it has frozen me to death.
such is the truth of my life;
i cannot comprehend.

SHAMELESS NOT

shameless.
i jerk all that shit inside out
in the crowd
out loud.
shameless.
i'm shameless just like you,
so i try my hand at rap
to tap the crap.
my head has spoken for so long
like a song
without a sound.
unbound, i throw these words up in the air
to make a stair
back to the one who sent me down
to the ground
to find a store
where heart is sold,
to find out
what's more gold—
the silence i keep,
or the words of soul.
i now roll
to take nothing back
coz it's crass.
all the bass,
it's a farce
to smother the bruises bruised,
to bring truce
to the fighting minds

that squander on drugs
sold in packets—
the seed of all rackets,
while i keep snorting
on love.
oh, boy, what joy this high is!
oh, boy what joy this lie is!
that makes me sell a world i don't have
to buy a world i cannot keep
coz it's deep.
these tears i weep
that drain down for no one to keep,
not a soul will know the blow
this heart takes,
how it shakes
the road when i jerk it out
coz i'm not shameless.
i'm not shameless like you.

SPOILS OF VICTORY

let us cross our lines of control,
take a stroll
into the minds of our foes,
and live the aftermath of a victory.
in their dream
it may last a few days and go on to years
depending on the size of ego they are feeding.
will the triumph feed the pride of their starving children?
will the glory shade the left over lives of the dead?
will some acquired piece of land limit the bounds of skies
that canvas aspirations beyond their walls?
will the war ever return the peace of pieces torn to patch
a net of devastation?
will ever the leaving breath not carry the scent of blood?
all this just a mere account the victor takes home,
and then you think where would the defeated take it
back to?

BALLOT

and i quote,
vote
be counted.
bring the mad men back to power.
let this circus run.
let the world see it play out yet again
the stunt inside the tent.
joke's on us.
in the audience,
the crowd will, thus, kill the crowd,
and a few men will be left to splurge the spoils.
don't toil,
yet
save the fight to quarrel
on everything that will go wrong
from now on
coz in the insides of our inside,
we both know
there are graver things to address.
this nation, our country,
can stay in mess
a little longer.
to hell with progress,
to hell with the decorum,
a single fart has to be flashed first
on a social forum.
come, let's vote our way to another misery,

ink our nails in pride,
share the burden,
elect our country
back into slavery.

BLIND COLOR

blessed are those whose sound is unaffected by light,
who have all but their ears to see.
for he who cannot see can surely hear the colors!
for there is nothing more pure than the sound of a voice
that has but his hands to see.
our dream but only lasts a night,
until that light
takes away all that we almost lived.
do not call him blind who cannot see.
shut your eyes for a moment,
you will thus see!

BOMBED

and so i've dried up the nights in making a bomb
whose wick,
i think,
i've ticked off some time back.
enough drama, or the lack of it, perhaps,
some bizarre clouds i've been talking to,
some moonlit stars,
my jar of scars,
and a room flooded with memories of future
predictions of my past.
a boat afloat
boarding the very present hours,
a product of my fear,
a wounded tear
must have laid the seed, perhaps.
i can tell you what makes me cry,
but it's never the same thing twice.
whilst the war battles this fight out,
i watch the wick burning out
closing in to burst.
i could also say 'explode',
but burst.
first things first,
i'm not a terrorist;
i intend no harm;
i'm just a madman
raring to burn this whole world
down on you.

YA ALI, MADAD

ya Ali,
this is how i spell strength.
ya Ali,
in my days of lent,
i've seen fear hide,
i've seen rainbow;
in tears, i've cried
each time i've muttered,
ya Ali, madad.

MIND THE WOODS

and i rumble
into the forest
with a wind behind the ruffling leaves
that crest on waves,
that bring scent of fresh dew,
brewed by tears of dream
of the night before.
will you walk by my side
stride for stride?
take a look into the woods
of my mind,
it's a jungle—
a torrid ransack of time,
burnt trees,
a stream riding on high tides,
birds chirping
in melancholy
of a long lost rhyme,
a stretch of barren land
reflects light,
a mirage of love bakes the sight
making a silhouette, though empty,
as pretty as fuck.
don't mind,
you are still inside.
collect the thorns
bleeding the pulp of frowning flowers
on your way back,
a souvenir of this desert once dense,
a story of future in past tense.

FOR THE WAR OF LOVE

it's late in the night now.
how many days should pass?
it's too late for a fight now.
guards down.
alas!
let's wage love, you and me,
show this world
how futile war is.
bringing death upon your enemy
can be such a relief
to him.
spread love, instead,
and then walk away
and watch it mix in the air.
and if it does not burn down
every single soul that breathes it,
come back,
pick that armor up again,
kill,
go back to war,
go do the humane thing.

FIREFLY

grafting peace, i leave the shore.
into the storm, i roar
to get lost,
to entangle.
a moment of peace
could cost me
a war,
wars even—
a price i am ready to pay.
cut my strings off.
let me dance.
burn down the wood.
let me lie.
fire me down.
give me the life
of a firefly.

REAL FICTION

find me a crowd that has a heart to hear things they do not want to listen,
and you shall find me naked of my solitude.
until then, wait for the silence that escapes the room
to smoke a delusion of probables,
and make a man of me in your ifs and buts.
i've given up on heart, mind, soul.
i have given up on the idea of life in whole.

SHAM

what a sham life is!
what truth death?
what devouring pleasure
thy seek?
what harvest
will be thy kin?
but the shade of trees
you sow,
no fruit will give you company.
when you go,
you go
alone.

ART YOU READY

yes, there will be art
in every era.
there will be words dripping in agony.
there will be paint that won't dry,
that which will speak about struggles of men,
that which may make you cry,
don't yet.
life has been fairly unjust to each one of us,
just wait for your turn!
if life had its way,
we'd all be dead.
instead,
here we are
collecting our bags of pain.
don't tell me i am sad;
i've been happier,
but it's no fun.
no light without water
can ever smear into a rainbow.
find out what hurts you
and cry, and cry, and cry,
until you cannot anymore.
if it doesn't make you art,
it will at least leave you a brush.

DON'T COVID THE FLOW

and i shove all that love inside the closet,
amidst the demons.
as i wait alone,
an eerie sense of calm,
i haven't felt in the recent past,
engulfs the air earlier smelling of fear.
as i rebuild watching the sunlight dance
on empty roads waiting for the stars,
dreams, unaware, splurge
while death smirks just a meter away.
wash your hand, sanitize;
my dreams have just sneezed on you.

RIHAYI

ki ab to bediyon pe zung chad gaya hai
rihaa kar de
ki ab khwabo ka zauf badh gaya hai
rihaa kar de
sazaa humne bhi kaati
tu bhi mujhse kuch kam qaid nahin tha
chal kaan pakadta hoon
nahin chhoonga tere bandon ko
zaamin hu teri hawao ka
ki hogi khushk kabhi
to bhigo dunga
meri kahani suna suna kar
ab bas bhi kar
rihaa kar de
ek aad mukamil waqt se saans kaat lu
peene de do ghoont gash ke
ki aa milu tujhse
ki ab sabr behad ho gaya hai
rihaa kar de

INSANITY

don't revere the insane;
some are just mad.
and there is nothing more crazier
than a mad man who knows
he is not mad.
this is crazy.
isn't it?
we are insane,
both of us,
but i'm not mad.

ONE DAY MATARAM

what is freedom
but the ability to love
without a purpose.
what is freedom
but the power
to hold on to secrets
without remorse.
what is freedom
but not having
your soul held
for a price.
but how far is the reach
of your liberty?
how much can we hurt?
is freedom then a selfish gift
or a charitable trust?

ART THIS

art is merely an honest extension of your subdued angst.
art is a solemn reflection of experience.
art is an extremely pious conversation with your maker—
the residue that remains as words or color on canvas,
that takes a life of its own
like a butterfly in the observer's mind.
art is a subject to start a talk,
to change,
to become.
art is a raging storm avalanching into the deepest part of you.
mark it untrue—all that pleasing pretentious material served in the name of art.
for if it does not want to make you go back to yourself and dig
your demons,
don't even start.

**

MOOD

tie me to either ends of the sky,
rip my flesh apart,
let me disintegrate to ashes,
let me start
again,
let me err,
let me sin,
let me seek God in the dark
and upon seeing him, shall i ask—
if that mind was enough for chaos
why make the heart?

DARPAN

kaun hai ye log aaine ke us taraf
ghar to akela hi lauta tha mein
aj phir ek aur raat zaaye hogi
inki mehmaan nawazi mein

AKS

aina dekhta hu
to na koi hasee dikhti hai
na koi bair
na dost
na dushman
bas ek ajeeb sa ladka budhape mein gum
nazar aata hai
kash kabhi selfie li hoti humne
is aks ka fareb pakda jaata

HUM

itne azad hue
ki khud mein kaid huye hum
itna bahein zameeno pe
ki sookh gaye hum
yun bhari udaan
ki aasmaan huye hum
jaati kahan hai ye raat
nikalta kaha se hai ye din
itne beshumar huye
ki suraj chaand huye hum
na jaat ka paath padha
na mazhabon mein bate hum
yun ghule mitti se
ki khud mulk huye hum

SEDATED

silence has been on sedatives since i last checked,
only to hallucinate her enough,
to dig out all she holds, she must.
how else do i always hear fading screams, riveting laughter, groans, and moans, when she is alongside me?
this silence...
she does hate light equally, coz i always see her around in the dark.
it takes me inside and inside of insides until it insinuates a lot of dream-like impossibles,
also called truth.
nights and her vibrating, resonating void, shows me pictures of love in vain, hurt, trembling in pain,
hiding, wanting to reach, strong enough to know it's weak,
waiting for nothing at all, yet yearing
also me.

ALL COLORS LIFE

and the strains of time devour on the restlessness of mind,
digressing into parts of us
that we have lived, that we will, that we are,
forging confusion,
the sane, though, never see it coming,
it takes horrible insanity to rationalize,
to understand that we perhaps have to just live
to find our God, before he finds us.
life, though, is just an idea, a layman's dream,
an affluent's abuse, a piety of the wise, a crafter's muse.
we can choose to skip a lane, walk in more comfortable shoes,
but our feet will leave no trail, our sweat won't get her dues.
go back, endure, become.
fate and faith are but words of play.
what has to come will come.

TURBULENCE

go to war, each of you;
there is more turbulence in peace.
find your enemy like your enemy found you.
hurt them, get hurt.
don't flee in cowardice,
for it's better to live with wounds
than to live in a space that hurts
but can't be seen.
choose void over a crowd of silence.
make them count
those bruises.
take it to your head when the heart cannot no more.
give birth to a clown;
there is nothing more terrorizing than laughter.
it kills who won't see your eye.
it will kill you all the same
coz you know this is all
but a lie.

i AM NOT US

nothing rots like a lonely mind.
nothing breathes fragrance like solitude.
where we are,
what we become,
is a walk we must tread on the lines of sanity.
this is for majority of the people, maybe, like me,
who are turning days and nights alike,
living pointlessly working hard,
manipulating our hearts into conceding strategies
of the mind,
of becoming nothing more than a body of life.
and then there are a few, maybe, like me,
completely insane,
who trespass boundaries of reasoning,
desiring a world of compassionate souls,
wanting to stride together,
to make this place around us we call our world,
which we have been gifted for no reason,
a more lovable place.
fighting the inevitable end,
we are so hell bent to prepone
coz we have to be the first
on the finish line of nowhere.
i am not crazy.
i am a crowd of souls.
but unlike you,
i know.

LONELY CROWD

where are we going with all this—
living constantly behind masks,
hiding so that we never meet ourselves?
in a dull moment, when all you got is you,
seek to seek more,
never to find.
we are all dirty, soaked in mud,
stinking of spent lives.
me and you,
we shall meet in hell one day
with our dearth of courage,
laughing at ourselves.
i see a lot
in the nights when the stars cry,
in the silences of the dark sky.
they've been around, they know,
man was made to live with men,
yet man was made to live alone.

FEET OF SKY

can we ever agree?
we don't have the same sky.
you see the blues,
i walk into them.
you hear the songs,
i paint words.
can we ever agree?
you dance in the storm,
i am it.
we are trees of the same bark,
but you sway more often
than i can shrug my roots off.
we are stars
of the same void,
but i am more empty than you.
we are not the same,
yet we love
when the toes of sky
get wet
in the raging waves
that leap in sigh.
how often have we agreed?
how often have you chose to walk away?
how often have the skies walked down in hope?
how often has the Earth sent her
steadily away?

SOME BARK AND BITE

the wolves have come to take my rotten soul.
i know.
i know.
i know.
can i hide behind this night?
can i dodge the end one last time?
i can, though,
run in, fight,
die;
but life waits
yet
for another try,
for one last time.
can i bring the sun down?
can i spend a little more time with my grief?
can i take my hurt and drown?
can i watch my last throw of dice?
if then i die,
i die.

WE ARE ALL MAD HERE

there is a mad man
inside me
waiting for light.
he can string his mayhem on
if it'd end.
how i've seen it unfold
the quirks of his sprawl,
it would be funny;
a joke for a joke,
a face for a face.
the madman and I
have switched our places
so often
it's been chaotic,
the order.
i don't know no more
if the madman is inside
at all.

SEVEN SHADES OF BLACK

what a treasure mind is!
how empty that heart!
how broken the soul must be that paints a rainbow
in the dark!
a wary sky
ripples
lightless
as i dream
a dream
of sleep.
what light must the broken pieces reflect
that the eyes must now weep?
love has lost her limbs and veins.
she, perhaps, has dug in too deep.
the stars will fall.
the dream will drown.
a flood will tear the sky,
my eyes,
your eyes,
and some truth in those lies.

A VOID THIS

void
is beautiful.
it is the unused Earth,
the empty light,
the pain,
the grief
that stays
beyond a laughter.
void
is magic.
it fills up spaces;
look carefully.
void
is a carnival
of pieces.
haven't you ever looked in an empty space
and seen your life dance?

DON'T

it gets lonely
once in a while,
in a crowd,
away from your thoughts;
it does get lonely.
nights reflect
and you feel cornered,
unable to deflect
the uneasy
shadows of truth,
and then a slight moment of weakness
pulls your vein
to a slit.
an awkward dullness
chokes your breath,
an uneasiness,
a responsive silence
brings the end
in those bleak moments
of utter confusion.
make a call to yourself.
read out the last note
you always wished to write.
i am the murderer;
this is not a suicide.

MANE MAN

wolves and beasts
and a pride to feed.
ugly and wounded,
dead bone deep,
nowhere to go,
no muscle to leap.
just a memory
of the past,
victor of grief.
a growl escapes
a tired heart
and the forest
hides.
they can keep
the trees.
they can keep
the streams.
the forest may
never be his again,
but the jungle?

POOR KING

art,
it empties
to fill.
there is nothing more
grief-stricken,
lonely,
real,
afraid,
poorer than art.
maybe, that's why
not all can afford.
we may glimpse
a parody
in color,
find remedy
in shades,
get lost even,
but to take art
inside you,
to let it
smear
every nook,
you must be
a king.

DREAM INN

don't shut your eye yet,
it may not be your dream.
sleep if you are ready
to see someone else's world.
and be ready to let go off your dream,
for someone may walk into
your streets of desire.
splurge your vice
and misery,
for someone may watch
your dreamy eyes
and every thing
you wanted to dream!
there is a new world
beyond that turn,
where you can rent a nightmare,
you may also lend a dream!
a cloud of secrets
with no one to claim,
we will live in different minds each night.
we will all live the same!

METRO DREAM

take a stride, fly;
we have road blocks
for now.
use the sky,
use my dream to boat;
i'll hop on to a cloud
nearby.
we are our own help,
our space,
our mind.
make a freeway
not bridges.
let's go back
in time.
this world
now calls for
roots.
the branches,
the trees,
the flocking leaves
can stand by
for now.
hop on to my dream;
i'll boat in a cloud
nearby.
love, the oldest poison known,
won't ever be an antidote.

but do you want to live at all?
are you willing to die
each moment
until the sky touches the ground?

i AM

i am that hell
that burns
night after night.
i am the price
love has paid
to stay.
i am all that hurt
and nothing more.
i am in my own pain,
and for all you
fools who think
i'm sad,
broken,
hopeless,
afraid,
i am!

ART SERVICE

art and her prejudice
make us dwell.
fire is never pretty,
even if painted in hell.
take it on face value,
you'd never know
the artist's fault.
what misery
must be his vice!
why did the brushes rub,
if they did?
why did the colors fall?
how much grief did it take
to leave the story abrupt?
how hurt were the eyes
that couldn't erupt?
how many lives did that art take
to paint such sorrow?
how much was the artist's fault?
how much did he borrow?

i OF THE STORM

the miracles are long gone,
and so is the curse.
darling, i am all by myself
with this life,
and i'm bloody hell at it.
no dream,
no sleep,
no courage left
to weep,
yet i stare back into the storm
in hope
to fool.
it's might...
she may have her
fists full.
she may bring her fury,
but i ain't going nowhere
when it's a fight,
it's a fight...

LURKING

write with smoke
in shadows,
the glory of this struggle.
no pride,
no days left
of the night
as i walk back
into the maze
one last time.
no strength left
for battle,
yet in the ring,
in the fight,
in blood stains
and pains,
in trophies
of grief,
i remain
dead
in the writings on the wall.
yet for glory,
i take the fall.
remember me
when they speak
of the king.
i may not have won
each time,
but i never left
the ring.

i am your fighter.
my paws,
smell of war,
come in, take that life,
come in, take what you've come for!

NOT TOLL FREE

i feel sorry for the people who are strong.
i am constantly afraid, anxious,
not that there is no faith;
i'm more God fearing than the angels.
i have seen it play in my head so many times
that it doesn't amuse me anymore.
there is no strength like the strength of allowing yourself
to be hurt.
i wish i could show you
the warm light that the pain soothes me with.
of course it breaks my bones too,
it doesn't let me sleep at night,
but how can i return him
an unscratched life,
an unblemished soul?
if he has to take me back,
i'll make sure
it's worth the toll.

PHIR SE

mujhko malum hai ki tujhko lagta hai
ki ye bhi har baar ki tarah guzar jayega...
shayad haan, mujhko malum nahi,
shayad tu akeli ho jayegi,
shayad main bhi, phir se

AWARA

jhagad mujhse
daant hi de
keh de
kyu du tujhe
teen din ki mohabbat ke badle
ta umar ka sukoon
par chod to tu bhi gayi hai
akela main bhi hu
thak kar kabhi
tere sirhane sar rakh ke soun
to gala zarur ghot dena
phir jhagadna mujhse
daant hi dena

PYASA

ab baat hui
to baat ho jaye gi
hum phir se chal padenge
na tere shikwe
na meri shikayat
magar aisi mohabbat kyu
kyu ye raat jab bhigoti hai
meri har saans
to teri saanse nahi rukti
kyu marti nahi tu
jab aankhein mili thi pehli baar
to aansuo se mulaqat hui thi
ab to rote bhi nahin
phir bhi jhankti hain
aisi sobat hui hai
inse
tu beshak roti hogi
mujko malum hai
par baat nahi karti
ke baat ho jayegi

SANGAM

par kisne likhi ye kahani
kisne chadhaye ispe nukte
kisne bhari inme khamoshiyon ki khusbu
kisne teri aankhon ke zabar
meri ankhon ke zer se bhare
kaun hai kirdar aakhir
tu?
mein?
ya kahani khud?

KAGAZ KE PHOOL

ek ravaayat karu
par tera dil baith jayega
ek kahani jo har raat
tapti hai
jalti hai
phir mayus hokar
thak kar
doob jati hai
ek aisi mohabbat
ki daastan
jo itni baar
mari hai
ki ab marti nahi
na chupti hai
na thakti hai
teri hasee
jise sungh kar
ye aankhen behekti hai
batati hai sabko
bitha bitha kar
ki kis aandhi mein
ungliya jalayi hain maine
kis sannato mein
tu aaj bhi kar rahi
hai intezaar
hum ne mohabbat zarur ki
tune mere khayalon se
maine tere ehsaas se
tu kalam ki siyahi ban kar

rang deti hai mere panne
main teri tasveero
mein nazm sa utarta hoon
safar ye saath katega
umar bhar
tu bhi jalegi paani ke der mein
main bhi bhigunga
beshak is aag mein
kya kya likhti hai
ye kalam mujhse
likh raha tha ek ravaayat
par dil baith gaya

SHREE CHAR SAU BEES

kabhi yunhi
na ho baat phir bhi
baat hoti hai
bolte bolte
kat ti hai raatein zaroor
magar na bolne ka jo din
guzarta hai
saalon sa lagta hai
aisa kyu karta hai
zulm ye waqt
bhag ta hai
chal padta hai kabhi
kabhi ruk jaata hai
tu
teri khushbu
jo itarti thi tere badan se
kabhi yunhi guzarta hu
mano puchti ho mujhse
aaj baat hui
haan hui dher sari
likha hai ek khat
awazon ka
lifafa bhi tera
pata likh chuki hai
ab hawa chale
to uda doon
phir se

DIL SE

agar tu
main hoti
aur main
tu
shayad mujhko
malum padta
tera dard
teri bebasi
tera darr
ghutan teri
sari
magar
tu kya
sehen
kar paati
tere yeh
faisle
teri
khamoshi
tera
ye suljha hua
pagalpan
main tujhko
shayad
bol deta
hai ab to
kya karu
nahi hai

tu mera
to kya
jaa maru
aur tu
bhaag jati
phir se
agar tu main
hoti
aur main
tu

DEEWANA

tera jism
jab chhuta tha main
ghav bharte the
mere
kuch aisa
jalta tha
tera badan
jaise sek raha
ho mera dard
ek raat hi to thi
phir kyu aisa
lagta hai
ki ek zindagi
bitayi
ho
tune
maine
jab doob
raha
tha suraj
to mohabbat
thi tujhse
ye raat
ne mujhko
tera bana
diya

DARR

tu hai to jaanta hu main
mar nahi sakta
na mohabbat ka ehsaas
na khushbu kahi
na rooh teri ab
na haatho ki narmi kahi
ek duniya tu le gayi
ek duniya mein
so rahe hain
jaagte bhi
kabhi yunhi
ujalo mein
taare gine kayi
khush hai tu
toh main kaise
par tu hai to jaanta hu
ki mar nahi sakta

RAVE

the demons wait for you to be alone.
that's how they hunt.
they wait and eat on your eagerness
to seek all that you wish you'd do
with not even your soul around.
and as you enter that room,
you always wanted to be in
to recover from the covert bruises,
to grieve,
to rejoice
in all that pain you gathered for this moment.
they sneak in, parade on your loneliness,
drink from the soul you knew was almost dead,
and push you deeper and deeper
into the middle of nowhere.
that's an address i now give you for their carnival,
for their feast on the human heart...
not all get there; some are plain unluckily happy.
for me, i am here now and everywhere to go,
but i choose to stay, get gnawed, and pick
whatever is left of me when i leave.
make no mistake, i won't leave a better man.
i will leave all the same...
life is not a fair draw;
some take the brunt and splurge,
some tip-toe on peace and fade away.
i have been dealt both: i am nothing and i am a world on my own.

WORLD VOID

void is home to genius
where all things chaos align
become peace
have a heart to live
with heart break
watch love
design
crafty spaces
of dream like
world
where everything that couldn't be
comes alive
courage,
a lot of it
should you choose
to live in void
gather your demons
make them a heaven
give them their
own asteroid

WE ALL FALL DOWN

the weaknesses of 4 ams
often met with prayers
seeking strength
to draw a sun
with perfect light
that burn away
the scars
afraid
drenched in guilt
not enough
soul left
to ask for some magic
to make it go away
the dirt of life
that runs your mind empty
into a dream
where you cannot sleep
good night, world
make a poem out of it
when you wake
and if you don't
show mercy
let me live
another day

- Just another strand she flutters that was kept unused, almost rusted, not to please herself or the onlookers; she called that just work.

- Not all that is written has to please her eye; sometimes I'm just honest.

- And in the woods, she leapt to an endless dead end... Spirit her light, grit her stick, fear her baggage, she would learn to trick

- That brute love drilled into the heart. O, war piece of art! No matter how much you pour now, no matter how much you roar, Like an uttered phrase, like a gutted gaze. It stays forever, even after it's gone.

- Short life; mine even shorter. Time has a knack for pacing the speed of seconds. Some just don't tick.

- And she left me with a device to do math. Maybe her way of showing two and two won't make five, but she counted out the one we cannot see.

- In straight hair and curls, in lack of sleep and rest, in famine and prosperity, in loneliness and in company, in walks and flights, in history and discoveries, in darkness and darkness in dreams and dreams until life does us part.

- Why me? Why not a rose that smells like a rose? Are you celebrating the fragrance of my shape, my color, my vigor to grow in places too shallow? I will wriggle, I will follow, and I will remain. What, after all, is there in a frame?

- A lot could have happened, but a lot did come to take a night, and I had to give. If we were anything close to what we are, a lot would have happened, but we weren't, and a lot did.

- There are dreams, and then there are dreams I dream and wish them to be untrue in the same breath! The world, I fear, is not ready for the circus!

- I do not follow, I stalk.
  I do not like, I lust.
  I do not comment, I judge.
  I am your invisible troll.

- When the barrage of words drown you, pick my silence to breathe.

- If love was the only wealth you could use to barter for food, clothes, and shelter, and death was a programmable function, where would your heart and mind be?

- I reflect different faces for different pair of eyes to see.
  I am no bird.
  I don't need no wings to fly.
  You do not have to set me free.

- Kabar toh phir bhi tera dahej hai
  Pehle zindagi se hui nizbat ka
  Tera haq adaa kar

- Ye kaisa ajeeb shoshan hua hai is daur ka
  Ke waqt chutkule suna raha hai
  Aur hass emoticon rahe hai!

- Tum mujhe unpadh do
  Main tumhe ghulami dunga

- Hisse aasmaan ke utne hi huye jitni lakeerein
  zameen pe khichi gayi
  Gar ho aukad durust toh humara hissa bhi le aana

- I can do a stand-up on grief, but who'd pay for such hilarity?

- Will you ever know which part was a dream? Don't sleep.

- Ke kitni bebas hogi ye kahani ke jab saath aate hai to grahan lag jata hai

- I wear a mask every day now, yet I know it's me.

- Traffic jams are directly proportional to emergencies. I have found myself on deserted roads, going nowhere.

- Won't I, for an I, actually make us see?

- Currently I'm dating myself, and I've never been in a more toxic relationship.

- Perception is one of the truths, like lies.

- Writing is letting a flood of emotion burn every muscle of your skin inside out to vaporize and then picking up the pen, knowing what to write not.

- The enormity of the circus inside is so fatal, all you can do is laugh.

- Tragedies are miracles that lost faith.

- Those who don't wander, often get lost.

You Write. We Publish.

THE WRITE ORDER

To publish your own book, contact us.

We publish poetry collections, short story collections, novellas and novels.

contact@thewriteorder.com

Instagram- thewriteorder

www.facebook.com/thewriteorder

www.ingramcontent.com/pod-product-compliance
Lightning Source LLC
LaVergne TN
LVHW010320070526
838199LV00065B/5614